How Many?

This book is for those who count, which is everybody.

First trade edition 2019
Copyright © 2018 by Christopher Danielson
All rights reserved, including the right of reproduction in whole or in part in any form.
Charlesbridge and colophon are registered trademarks of Charlesbridge Publishing, Inc.

At the time of publication, all URLs printed in this book were accurate and active.
Charlesbridge and the author are not responsible for the content or accessibility of any website.

Published by Charlesbridge
9 Galen Street
Watertown, MA 02472
(617) 926-0329
www.charlesbridge.com

First published in 2018 by Stenhouse Publishers • www.stenhouse.com

Library of Congress Cataloging-in-Publication Data
Names: Danielson, Christopher, author.
Title: How many?: a different kind of counting book/Christopher Danielson.
Description: First trade edition. | Watertown, MA: Charlesbridge, 2019. |
  Series: Talking math
Identifiers: LCCN 2018047999 (print) | LCCN 2018057376 (ebook) |
  ISBN 9781632898135 (ebook) | ISBN 9781632898142 (ebook pdf) |
  ISBN 9781580899437 (reinforced for library use) | ISBN 9781580899451
  (soft cover)
Subjects: LCSH: Counting—Juvenile literature. | Mathematics—Juvenile
  literature. | Counting—Study and teaching (Elementary) |
  Mathematics—Study and teaching (Elementary)
Classification: LCC QA113 (ebook) | LCC QA113 .D37227 2019 (print) | DDC
  513.2/11—dc23
LC record available at https://lccn.loc.gov/2018047999

Printed in China
(hc) 10 9 8 7 6 5 4 3 2 1
(sc) 10 9 8 7 6 5 4 3 2

Display type set in Myster Bold by Denis Serebryakov
Text type set in Grenadine MVB by Markanna Studios Inc.
Printed by 1010 Printing International Limited in Huizhou, Guangdong, China
Production supervision by Brian G. Walker
Designed by Joyce White
Photography by Scott Dorrance (www.dorrancestudio.com)
Food styling by Lorie Dorrance (www.loriedorrance.com)

TALKING MATH

CHRISTOPHER DANIELSON

How Many?

A DIFFERENT KIND OF COUNTING BOOK

Charlesbridge

This is a book about **numbers** and **counting**, but it's different from other counting books.

This book **doesn't** tell you what to count.

It **doesn't** start with small numbers and end with big ones.

Instead **you decide** what to count on each page. You have many choices.

The longer you look, the more possibilities you'll notice.

TURN the page to see for yourself.

Look at this picture.

How many
do you see?

If you thought, "How many **what** do I see?" then you get the idea.

Maybe you'll **count the shoes**. There are two of those. Or maybe you'll count **pairs of shoes**. There's one of those.

There is one box, but how many **shoelaces**? How many **holes** for the laces to go through? (Those are the eyelets.) How many **ends** on the laces? (Those are the aglets.)

Maybe you'll count the **yellow stitches**, or something completely different.

What other things can you count?

Now how many do you see?

This book is filled with **sets of pictures**. Within each set you'll find many things to count. Some things **change**. Some things **stay the same**. Some things might **surprise** you.

Ready to start counting?

TURN
the page.

How many?

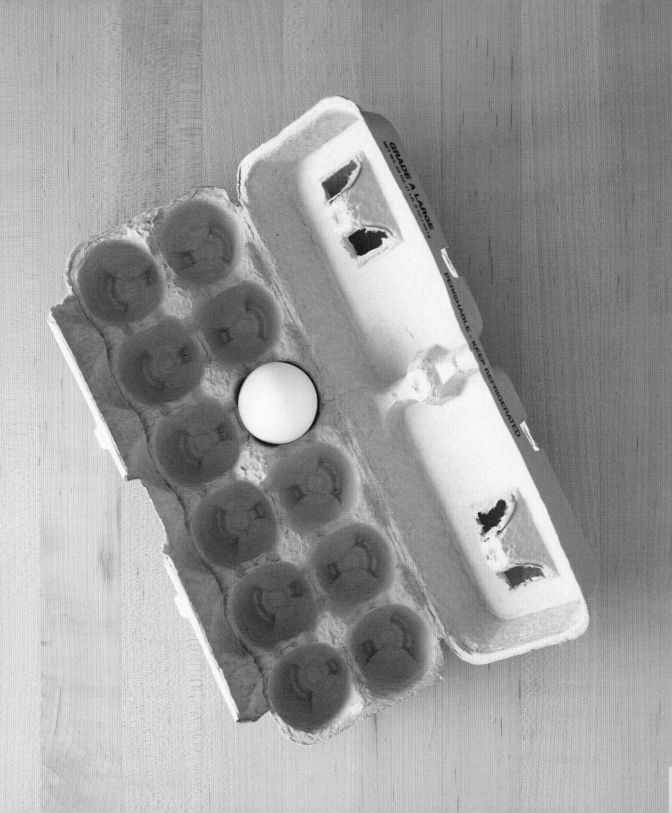

How many?

How many?

How many?

How many?

How many?

How many?

How many?

How many?

How many?

How many?

How many?

Once you've read this book a few times, you might think of new questions to wonder about:

What's the **largest** number in this book?

What's the **smallest** number?

What number is most **surprising**?

What's your **favorite** number? Can you find that many of something on **one** of the pages? Can you find it on **every** page?

What numbers are **missing**?

Your world *is* full of interesting things. Go count them!

Dear Reader,

Have fun counting. Look closely. Notice new things.

If you think you can't compare apples and oranges (or in this case grapefruits), remember they are both kinds of fruit.

Relationships are important. Two shoes make one pair. Twelve eggs make one dozen. Fifteen avocado halves make one big batch of guacamole.

When you count carefully and clearly state what you're counting, you're doing some great math!

—Christopher